D1785746

The Rebirth of Love

The Journey to Self-Love

Maryam Yousaf

Muslima Today Publishing

Muslima Today Publishing

www.muslimatoday.com

DEDICATION

To the one who taught me what true love is, to the turner of hearts – Al Wadud (God) The Loving One. And to all those who deserve to know what love really is and where it truly belongs. To those who are being called back home – to the home of your heart and to the owner of all hearts – Allah (God).

INTRODUCTION

The greatest love second to God and his beloved Prophet (peace be upon him) is the love of one's self.

Self-love is the acceptance of one's own flaws and weaknesses, heartbreaks and mistakes, experiences and lessons. It is the love and nurturing of your own body, mind and soul.

Loving one's self is the refusal to be dependent on someone else's love. Refusing to wait for someone else to value your worth, before doing so yourself. Despite the world doubting you; never doubting yourself. Loving yourself unconditionally for who you are and what you have been through.

In your quest of love perhaps you may have tragically ended up losing your sense of self. Self-love is a journey to rediscovering yourself and reconnecting to your soul.

Self-love is having the beautiful ability to let go of the heart wrenching events and experiences that have ever happened to you by giving yourself the hope and love to heal. It's about refusing to talk negatively to yourself but instead treating oneself as a true best friend, an encourager, motivator and inspirer.

Self-love is never giving up on yourself and always striving to be better, it is about forgiving yourself for the mistakes you have made.

Self-love is about being compassionate and kind to yourself. It is about providing yourself with all the love you deserve, the love you so desperately looked for in others, the love that makes you feel at home. It's a powerful path to self-healing and self-development that only you can do by yourself for yourself.

Self-love is like a barrier you wrap around yourself, a barrier which prevents negativity. It is a barrier so powerful that it protects you from your own inner-demons. Self-love is a super power which can transform your whole outlook on life and bring you the love and healing you so desperately need. It makes you feel invincible because God is with you. You become firmly rooted in the ground and no wind or rain can shake you.

Throughout our life, we search and even expect someone else to hold our hand, but the one hand we need to hold onto and never let go of is our own. I have therefore written this book on self-love comprising of memoirs, stories, poems and quotes to remind myself and remind you of this. I no longer want you or I to get lost in the pursuit of the things we think will make us happy.

Happiness starts within, please remember this.

Let the torch of self-love shine bright within.

Welcome to the beginning of your journey to Self-Love

PAINFUL MEMORIES

People become heart-broken thinking it is because of someone else. Someone might have broken our hearts once, but by replaying these painful memories we continue the hurt and pain by breaking our own hearts every day.

When we feel heartbroken we blame and give full responsibility to others. However, we fail to take responsibility for breaking our own heart repeatedly! Through negative self-talk and by constantly judging ourselves through the eyes of others instead of our own. There is only one person that can make you feel happy and that is you.

So, learn to love yourself and keep yourself safe from bad feelings and dark thoughts, keep yourself from breaking your own heart.

IT'S TIME

It is time you discovered all the love within you.

It is time for you to know that if you have yourself then you will be much happier and stronger and you *my dear* will thrive.

It is time for you to understand that the lesson you must learn from all your negative experiences is that you must love and respect yourself.

You will continue to be disappointed if you expect the love you need to come from others. People may give you love but it can never equate to the love you can give to yourself. You see giving yourself love is what makes you free, free from need, free from fear.

If you have self-love then you have self-belief, resulting in unimaginable power and confidence. When you attain this level of success then it's almost *impossible* for anything or anyone to break you.

BESTFRIEND

Become your own best friend, and you won't stand for any negativity from yourself or anyone else.

Take some quiet time and connect within to become more mindful of who you are. You will see the world differently; you will care about yourself before caring about what others want you to do.

Appreciate who you are and all the unique qualities that make you, you. This will help you with spiritual growth. It will help you to accept your weaknesses better and your strengths. You will start to take better care of your basic needs. You will become protective of yourself which will make you respect yourself even more. You will be able to become more compassionate to yourself so you can truly reach your true potential in all aspects of life.

Having a best friend with you all the time means *always* having someone there to motivate you, to make you laugh and to cry with you. You can heal because you are not alone, you have all the love and support you need from your best friend. Hence, during the delicate moments of loneliness in your life, you will not feel lonely, because it's like having two of you in one body, you and your best friend. *Therefore, become your own best friend, and become it now.*

REBIRTH OF LOVE

Losing the love of your life is almost like grieving their death, *worse* than that is to lose yourself. However, find the courage to stand tall by being there for yourself. Talk and listen to yourself, slowly heal and pray, every day. You will be able to let go of the pain and live for yourself.

This is the *rebirth of love*, when you discover the beauty and worth of your inner-self.

I CHOOSE ME

Say this prayer with me: Today I choose not to die one more time while I try to bring my lost love back to life. Today I make the decision to prioritise myself and not compromise my life. *Today I choose me.*

MY GIFT TO MYSELF

Your gift to yourself is to unconditionally love and accept all your imperfections and flaws, and to always stand up for yourself even if it's in silence.

SWIM

Swim in love but do not allow yourself to drown.

STARS

They weren't scars but a collection of important lessons she had picked up along the way. It was her very own map of stars that she shared with the sky that followed her. The shining trophies of all life's conquests.

ACCEPTANCE

We are always looking for a happy ending, for some type of closure. As if our life is not complete without it. We search in all the wrong places for something that we can only find deep within our self. We seek the acceptance from others which we can only give to our self. We mistakenly give away to soon all our love, time and energy so easily to the wrong people, the love that we owe to our self and then wonder why we feel so empty?

We expect everything to make sense and ask never-ending questions. We put our lives on pause by always over thinking.

But life goes on. Accept that some things will never make sense. Accept what was and carry on living and moving forward. Make your love and relationship with God your *strength* and soon you won't be carrying mountains but *moving* them instead.

PEACE

When you find God, you find your purpose, you find yourself and you find peace.

VALIDATION

Value yourself and you won't ever need anyone else to validate you.

YOU ARE WHO YOU ARE AND NOT WHAT IS SAID ABOUT YOU

If someone tells you 'You are a millionaire' does that instantly make you into a millionaire? If someone tells you 'You are 6ft' do you automatically go from 5ft to 6ft? No, right? In the same way, you do not become ugly when someone calls you ugly. It does not make you unlovable when someone calls you unlovable. It does not make you nothing just because someone says you are nothing.

So, stop catching every negative comment that is thrown at you. *Words do not make something true.* Sometimes the cruel things that people say, they say to hurt you, to dominate you, to make you feel unworthy, because they do not want you to see your self-worth. They get angry by seeing you as the incredible person that you are, so their tactic is to break your confidence. Once you start doubting yourself they no longer feel threatened by your presence.

However, some people will tell you exactly what you need to hear, even if you don't like it. To find out which one is which, you must sincerely reflect and scrutinise your actions to ensure you are not in the wrong. However, a person that advices you with concern and love will not talk down at you but speak with compassion.

ALIVE

We think we cannot live without some people,
perhaps this is the lesson we learn by losing them.
We can live and we will. We do not need anybody
else to stay alive but ourselves.

PARTS

Sometimes parts of us only truly come alive when other parts of us die.

YES

One persons NO is somebody else's YES. Every time you are faced with rejection be happy that you are one step closer to your true destination. Which is where you truly belong and exactly where God wants you to be.

SURVIVOR

You are not the bad things that happened to you.
You are a survivor of the chaos that you were tested
with. You are a warrior that has come out stronger
on the other side.

IT IS NOT YOUR FAULT

When we are betrayed, disrespected or unappreciated by those who we love we start to blame ourselves. We blame ourselves for someone else's behaviour. The behaviour that has nothing to do with us.

So please hear me and believe me when I tell you it is not your fault. It is not your fault if you were betrayed. It is not your fault if you were disrespected. It is not your fault if you were unappreciated. It is not your fault if you were cheated on. It is not your fault so please believe it and say it with me – It is not my fault.

FIERCELY YOU

Shift the energy from caring about what other people think of you to what you think of them. How it makes them feel to be around you- to what it makes you feel to be around them.

When you focus on how you feel then you inherit the confidence to be yourself. This is when you will realise your own happiness comes first, you will acknowledge the importance of your own comfort. This is when you unapologetically and fiercely become the true you.

YOU ARE YOU

People's opinion of you is not who you are. You are who you are. If you are a beautiful person, you are a beautiful person. What people say cannot change that.

The way people treat you cannot change that. If you are a good person, people's false rumours cannot change that.

You will always have control of who you are if you do not let people's opinions dominate you.

If you are secure in yourself, you will be happy no matter what is said about you. If you distinguish who you are from how people see you, then no one can steal your peace.

THE LOVE WITHIN

You need to find the love within you before you look anywhere else.

EVERYTHING

It is not relationships with others that make you feel complete; it is the relationship between God and oneself. Once you have that special connection with your Creator, everything else will fall into place. Because you cannot complete what has already been completed. If you have God and a special connection with yourself then that is everything.

ALL THE LOVE

All that love you have to give, there is no one more deserving of it than you. The reassurance you seek from others can only come from you.

THE OCEAN OF LOVE

Nurture the ocean of love that flows inside you.

SPREAD THE LOVE

Spread love and you will feel love.

SEE YOURSELF

People will see you in the way you see yourself. Respect yourself and others too will respect you. If you disrespect yourself or have no value for yourself, then no one else will either. Nobody wants someone that is desperate for love and attention.

The more you run after some people the further they will run from you. You seek love from all the wrong places. Respect yourself enough to walk away from someone that does not want you. Value yourself enough to know where you belong and where you do not.

Love yourself and give your love to God and it will never be wasted.

LET GO

How can you blame someone for not loving you?
When you cannot blame yourself for loving them?
Love is sometimes in no person's control. It is
never forced. If someone cannot love you it does
not mean there is a defect in you. It is what it is.
So, respect the rejection and *if you truly love
someone*, then let them go.

BODYGUARD

Surround yourself with positivity and self-love. Be your own bodyguard against hateful speech and low self-esteem. Every time a negative thought occurs say *'no'* that is not me and immediately seek refuge in God from the evil whispers of the devil.

THE SHIELD OF LOVE

Hold up the shield of love when they throw the stones of negativity at you. Refuse to let them break you. Block the negativity from penetrating within by guarding yourself with the mirror of reflection. Their poisonous words reflect the venom inside them. Their words define them, not you. Just remember it has nothing to do with you.

So, guard yourself with the shield of love and *God-willing* their words will not harm you.

FIND YOURSELF

If you feel lost, then give the feeling of belonging to someone else. If you need help, then help someone else. You will feel lighter and happier.

Helping others benefits us in more ways than we could imagine. It brings out the potential that we did not know we had, the potential to do *great* things.

THE DESTINATION OF LOVE

We may need to unlearn everything we thought we knew about love, so we can learn the true meaning of what it is. What love is, and what it is not. Perhaps this is the blessing we collect through the journey of a thousand heartbreaks; to discover the true essence of receiving and giving love. So that we can recognise it and never mistake it for anything less than it is. Through this long powerful journey we reach the true destination of love. The love which leads back to God and to the sacred connection to our soul.

THE ROLLERCOASTER FROM HELL

We enabled them with our empty threats. We allowed them to continue the cycle of abuse, we accepted the disrespect.

We enabled them by making them think we would always be there. They never thought we would eventually gain the courage to jump off the rollercoaster from hell.

But we did, and now we are stronger than we ever were before. And just as a mother protects her child, we protect our heart and soul. We learnt to give our self the love we were deprived from.

Finally we are free, because we had the strength to escape all the insanity. *So praise God, The Almighty.*

WHEN

Question: When will he pay for what he has done?

Answer: When you stop caring.

BEAUTY AND THE BEAST

You are not crazy, you are just so deep in love.
You have been attacked, yet you still stay- hoping
for better days. But my darling, this is not love, this
is a mess. This cycle will never end until you are
brave enough to do something about it. Be gentle to
your soul, you do not deserve this pain.

Do not be afraid of being alone, have you not
heard? Those who have no one, have God.

You have the power to stop this oppression. Do
what you need, seek help from where you can find
it and flee from this aggression. My darling for the
sake of your life, for the sake of your sanity please
help yourself. I know it is terrifying but you can do
this.

You are a beauty that should not have to put up with
a beast.

Set yourself free from the emotional turmoil. Do
not fear the one that does not fear God. Make
prayer and cry out to your Lord, complain to Him.
Your condition will not change until YOU change
it. Please make a decision and put your trust in
Him. God will surely lead you out of darkness into
light, keep your faith in Him.

SHACKLES

She stopped tying her feelings to one person. She stopped building homes in people. She discovered the reality. She untied the devils knot and freed herself from the shackles.

LOVE YOURSELF

People cause pain. At times it is intentional, at other times it is not. Do not concentrate on their words and horrible actions. However, concentrate on your reaction. Unfortunately, we are often quick to engrave the heart-breaking words someone has stabbed us with and for some foolish reason accept it as the truth.

Please do not get caught up in the mind games that people play. Speak to yourself with love and respect. Defend yourself when these horrible words haunt you and tell yourself that it is not true. Learn to speak positively to yourself, with love and compassion.

If you do this then there will come a day when you see the person that had caused you so much anguish, grief and sorrow, *and you will not feel anything*. This is because what they think, feel or say will no longer matter to you.

The only thing that will matter is what you think, feel or say- about *yourself*.

ADDICTION

You should never beg for someone's love and you should never have to. Do not question why someone did not love you but ask yourself why you even wanted that kind of love, the love that was cold as ice and gave you nothing but pain and poisoned you with heartache. That was not love, it was an addiction that had robbed you of yourself.

NARCISSIST

I ignored myself for far too long, I turned a blind eye and a deaf ear to the cries of my soul. I silenced the voice in my head. My heart was screaming for help, the sirens signalling pain, yet I ignored it again and again. I was made to feel crazy, and guilty. When I finally had the courage to question you, all I got was your silent treatment.

Why were you so angry? My life was just a game for you.

I thought I was to blame but really it was the narcissism in you that was feeding off my pain. I now take back all my love; the love you didn't deserve, and I give it to myself. This love belongs to me. I have put it away so deep within my soul because I do not want to be betrayed again by someone like you. As I throw you out of my life, I grow in love for myself and apologise to my heart, body and soul for dragging them through hell and I promise never to do it again.

LOVE IN HER EYES

What is it I can see in your eyes? Is it love, at last?
It has been a long time coming but I am *so happy*
that you have found yourself. You must promise
never again to let yourself go, *not for anyone*.

FLASHBACKS

To my heart, I am happy to tell you that I am back again. For a while I had gotten lost in the flashbacks, in the memories. But my love I want to tell you that I am back again after overcoming the obstacles. Please pull me back and hold me close if you feel I am getting lost again. Sometimes sadness tries to overtake me, all I need is for you to pull me back home.

THE PROBLEM

She said she thought of many people but she did not think of herself. You see, that is the problem, we *always* put ourselves last.

TRUE LOVE

True love is to love your own self. Not everyone is capable of giving true love because they do not possess a pure and loving heart. We always give so much of ourselves to everyone else but we often put ourselves last. Mistakenly we believe it is someone else's job to love us, but it is not. We need to put ourselves first and put our broken hearts back together by the help of God.

THE WOMAN IN THE MIRROR

I am so proud of the woman she has turned out to be. She is the woman in the mirror smiling back at me. She has conquered all her fears and resisted the arrows and swords. The words of God are her fortress.

TODAY

Someone needs you today, to wipe their tears away.

Someone needs you today to pray for their healing, guidance and relief.

Someone needs you today to remind them that they are loved and worthy of the love they desire.

Someone needs your care, love and affection to remind them that everything will be okay.

Someone needs you today, that someone is *you.*

TWO MADE OF ONE

You are two made of one. A beautiful body and a strong soul.

TO THE LOVE IN ME

I have spent my whole life looking for you, but you were here with me all along.

THE UNIVERSE

You are chasing the world when you have the whole universe inside you.

RECONNECT

Perhaps the pain will leave when you have learnt the lesson you so desperately need to learn. First you must reconnect deeply with your soul to discover a whole new hidden universe.

THE AWAKENING

One day your eyes will be awakened and you will be able to see things for what they really are. It will feel as though you have been blind and at last you can see again. It will be the day you have learnt the lesson, the day you finally understand why events unfolded in the way they did. It will be the day when you no longer burn with pain, it will be the day you will be *free* once again.

THE BEGINNING

One day you will look back and laugh. You will laugh at all the things that you cried over and thought you could not live without. You will separate yourself from the person you once were and it will be as if you are looking back at someone else *who was she?* You will ask yourself.

You will grow up to be a wonderful person that can conquer the world. And you will be able to laugh at the things which you cry over now, because you will realise how insignificant some things were, what seemed to be the end of the world was just the beginning.

SELF-TALK

When someone else hurts us we may refuse to put up with it and walk away. But why do we continue to hurt our own self by dwelling upon the past? Why do we relive the most painful episodes of our life every night? We commit suicide by reliving the pain.

It's so important to love ourselves. To maintain positive self-talk and to be good to ourselves. Deep down we know we are valuable and important.

Therefore, we must seek refuge in God and remember Him so He will remember us. Seek refuge in Him so He can protect us from the secret whispers of the devil who works so hard to destroy our souls. The next time the devil comes to you with negative self-talk, *knock him out* by seeking refuge in God.

ME, MYSELF AND GOD

From the beginning until the end, it's me, myself and God.

REJECTION

Facing rejection is difficult. *"Why does he not like me?"* or *"Why was I not good enough?"* These are just some of the questions we obsess about. What we need to understand is that the ones who rejected us never had any control over their hearts. You see it is only God who controls the heart.

You can never make anyone love you if God has not allowed that person's heart to love you. You can never be a part of someone's life no matter how much you want it, if it's not written for you. It is a test and we must have patience and trust that God has something better planned for us. No matter how painful it is we must accept the things that are out of our control and thank God for protecting us from all the things we have no knowledge of.

All we need to understand is what God does, He does for the best. *Trust Him.*

HOLES

People make holes in the heart. Seeking self-love through God makes the heart whole again.

THE PREVENTION

The biggest lesson you will learn is to never completely give yourself to anyone except God. Once you have God, you will love yourself. This is the prevention and cure from a million heartbreaks.

SELF-HATE

I have learned- those who hurt me did so because they too were hurting deep inside. They needed to project that self-hate and inflict their negativity and despair onto someone else. They desired to break the strong because *they* were weak.

They could not bare to see me happy because their insecurity and jealousy was killing them inside. Somehow it made them feel better by trying to destroy what was mine. I was the one who gave my everything- just to make them smile, all the while they plotted, slandered and lied.

I was given no option but to walk away from the mess and chaos.

I learned I could not save the people that did not want to be saved.

I learned that not everyone you help wants to be helped, some people will just pull your hand to drown you with them.

I learned that sometimes the best thing you can do is pray and walk away because sometimes that is all you can do.

FREE

You can try to hurt me or my reputation as much as you like. In the end, I will always be me. There is nothing you can do to stop or change who I am and that is what sets me free.

BE YOURSELF

When we hear that someone has said something unjustified about us it is easy to feel low and to start behaving differently towards the people who listened to these rumours. But my advice is to be strong, and to be yourself. Ignore the hateful lies or rumours and show people who you really are. Your best weapon is you, do not hold yourself back. Allow people to experience your joyful and kind nature. Always be your wonderful self especially when people least expect it.

YOU AND GOD

When people keep breaking your trust and you no longer have anyone to rely on, don't' worry but be happy. See the good in this, which is, you will learn to only rely on yourself and on Allah. And that is when you will become independent from the creation and only dependent on your Creator. Relying on yourself, on God and no one else makes you powerful not weak.

REMIND

Remind yourself why you left.

Remind yourself how lonely you felt and how much your heart hurt every day you were with him.

Remind yourself why you chose yourself over him.

Remind yourself that you finally figured out you were better without him and it just was not meant to be.

Do not waste your life chasing after what you ran away from.

Remind yourself to not fall into his mind games.

Remind yourself to not go around in circles by trying to fix what will always stay broken.

Take control of the situation and take control of your life.

Remind yourself that you deserve better and you are worthy of a love that is loyal and true.

Remind yourself until you do not need to remind yourself again of your self-worth.

FINDING YOURSELF

One of the most important journeys of your life is
the journey of finding yourself. To do this you must
first find God. Only then will you be strong enough
to handle any storm with a smile.

FAILURE

Failure taught me to be patient with myself, to be patient with time. I realised failure was a blessing. There are blessings in everything; we just need to open our eyes to see.

THE SEARCH

We are all searching for something, but in the end we realise we do not need anything else but belief in ourselves and trust in God.

THE MOST BEAUTIFUL GIRL IN THE WORLD

You might be the most beautiful girl in the world, however if the one person whose opinion matters to you the most reserves only criticism for you it might feel like the opposite. Do not doubt yourself, do not question your beauty. Those who make you feel inferior want to manipulate and make you believe that you are not good enough for them, so that you don't leave them.

Surround yourself with the people *who make you feel good*, people who *encourage* you to be better, who *help* you to realise your self-worth and bring you *closer* to God. These are the people you deserve in your life, the ones who do the opposite *do not deserve you.*

WHY DO THEY HATE ME?

"Why do they hate me? What did I ever do to them?" Have you ever asked yourself these questions?

Many pure hearted people are hated on because negative people cannot comprehend the innocence and love that oozes from good people's hearts and actions. They judge good people by their own evil intentions and falsely believe they have a hidden agenda just as they do. Sometimes they hate you because they secretly desire to be you or to have you. So, if it appears that someone hates you for no apparent reason, do not feel sad. They want to make you feel paranoid and unworthy.

The reason you have their attention in the first place is because they *know* you are good enough. They will try to bring you down by portraying an ugly image of you to other people. All you have to do in this situation is to continue to be your *fabulous* self.

STORMS

You have always been strong, you have just had to battle a few storms to realise it.

CATCH YOURSELF BEFORE YOU FALL

Every now and then, someone will become a part of your life. You will come to love them, but they will eventually break your heart. Whether its family or friends, you will realise you cannot really trust anyone completely, *except yourself and God.* Therefore, prepare to catch yourself before you fall. Heartbreak can be devastating and it comes without warning. Do not let it destroy you, turn to God and to your inner-strength.

DARLING

Sure, you can find 'the one' with time but darling
first, find yourself.

SUCCESS

Not everyone has the same opportunities in life. Do not look at others and think you cannot reach their level of success. Make the most of the opportunities you do have, God-willing you will get your own success. Not everyone was made to be the same. We all have a purpose, and our own individual strengths so *do not ever forget that*.

BE BETTER

Do not be bitter, be better. You have *so much* to be thankful for.

Be better because you have experienced the beauty of vulnerability which takes you a step closer to God.

Be better because you have made it through alive.

Be better because you have learnt lessons that make you powerful and experienced what has made you wise.

Be better because you have a better life, because you are a brand-new person.

You will realise all of this in time.

Be better because better things are coming your way.

TRANSFORMATION

Your transformation will take you from the ground to the sky. You no longer care about what people think of you, your primary concern is your own and God's opinion of you.

When you reach this level of security and confidence, welcome yourself to recovery, to the real freedom.

ATTACHMENT

When your heart, body and soul are screaming to break away, attachment is what keeps you chained. Initially, detaching yourself from this entrapment will cause great pain.

The pain may be unbearable, similar to the pain of a useless limb being amputated from the body. No matter how painful the procedure it must be done for survival.

Therefore, amputate those attachments which will one day poison your life in this world, and the next. It will hurt, but you will heal one day, like others before you did.

You have more to gain than to lose.

DON'T GIVE UP

Don't ever give up on yourself. Rather than focusing on your failures, focus on your strengths and *everything* you can achieve.

Do not let your sins hold you back.

Let your faith drive you forward.

FORGIVENESS

Forgive others so that *The Exceedingly Forgiving* (God) may forgive you. Forgiveness relieves the bricks of tension and anxiety that have built a barrier in your heart. All it takes is a moment of forgiveness to break down these barriers and to acquire the peace your soul has been longing for. Let forgiveness free you from all those years of imprisonment.

Be yourself once again by *letting go* of all the things that take away your inner-peace.

FIRST STEP

Take the first step to self-love even if it's just smiling at yourself.

TEARS

We must let go of the idea that the same people who are responsible for our tears will give us back our smiles.

INTENTIONS

Not everyone has the same heart or the same intentions as you. The sooner you learn this, the stronger you will be.

NEVER LOSE HOPE

To feel complete, you do not require someone else's acceptance. You need your own love and acceptance.

No matter how people treat you, you do not allow it to define your self-worth. You are good as you believe yourself to be.

So, start believing in yourself and *never* lose hope.

BROKEN PIECES

How I wish I could take all your broken pieces and hug them back together again. But only you can do that by taking one step closer towards God.

Renew your intentions and be serious about moving forward with your life.

Holding onto a memory will not take you back in time. Some things were already dead before you saw them die.

It is time to face the truth and heal yourself because you are a pure loving soul who deserves the very best.

KEEPING IT REAL

The most precious relationship is the one where you can completely be yourself in (without any fear of being rejected). That's when you know it's real.

ALONE

It is better for you to be alone than to be with the wrong person. If they make you feel miserable all the time it is a damaging attachment which you need to be released from. *It is not love.*

PRAYERS

Your prayers and love for yourself are your very own bodyguards, keep them close and never be without them.

I LOVE ME

I do not need everyone to love me. God loves me and I love me, that is enough for me.

GODS GIFT

How can I say my body and face is ugly? I promise to love it and be gentle and kind to this beautiful gift from God which has been entrusted to me.

EXCEPTIONAL

You are being tested; you will come out stronger than you thought was possible. So, endure patiently with prayer and embrace this change which will transform you to be the person God wants you to be; an exceptional human being.

HEALING

A part of healing and moving on is learning to embrace the pain.

GOOD ENOUGH

I am good enough. I will not doubt myself based on a person's negative opinion. My face, skin and my height is beautiful. I am beautiful. I love and accept myself exactly the way I am. The person that deserves me and is worthy of my commitment, my time and my love will accept me for myself. Anyone who does not is frankly not good enough for me.

TURN THE TABLES

Switch the question from 'Am I good enough?' to, 'are they good enough for me?'

THE FACTS

It didn't work out. Not because you weren't good enough but because it was just not meant to be. So, stop overthinking and accept the facts. You are worthy of true love and you are good enough for the person that deserves you, the person that has been written for you. So be patient and do not break your own heart.

SOMEONE SPECIAL

If they make you feel bad about yourself, it's not fair on you and you don't deserve to be treated that way. We all have flaws, but the one who constantly brings you down at every given opportunity is not your friend, or soul mate.

You need someone that will fall in love with your flaws, and will make you feel special, valued, appreciated and loved.

...someone that will make you *laugh,* not cry

...someone that will bring out the *best* in you, not the worst

...someone that is *happy* the way you are, not someone who constantly compares you to others

...someone that will *encourage* you to get closer to God, not someone who will drag you into sin

You deserve someone special who will love you just the way you are. Do not give anyone permission to mistreat you or make you feel as if you are not good enough. If something is bothering you, communicate and give things a chance to improve. Some people have no awareness of where they are going wrong. Perhaps a deep and meaningful conversation will fix everything.

YOUR HAPPINESS

People that like to make others happy often forget about their own happiness, their own dreams and goals. They often sacrifice their own happiness for the sake of someone else. They are too busy taking care of everyone else's needs that they forget to take care of their own need to be happy.

The same people they give all their attention to are often ungrateful and see this wonderful gift of giving as a weakness (because they would never do the same in return). So, they start to view this special ability of giving as something that is owed to them, something that you will never deserve for yourself. They almost start demanding your life. If you dare mention that you have a desire to do something for yourself then they will tell you, no, and not to even think about yourself, well not yet, not until they can dispose of you themselves. 'Put me first and put yourself last as you have always done'.

However, stick to your values and give without expectation but do not ever stop giving to yourself. Make a promise to yourself that you will give yourself more. Go out of the way for yourself, make yourself happy, and achieve your own dreams and goals just as you would do for others. Promise to never leave yourself behind.

If you do not think of yourself, no one else will.

REMINDER TO MYSELF

Just the way I go out of my way to help others, I will go out of my way to help myself.

MYSELF

I gave myself the love you didn't deserve.

IF YOU ONLY KNEW

If you only knew God the way He should be known. To even begin to grasp His love for you will be enough to make you happy.

You need to deeply reflect on what you want from this life, the love of people or the love of God?

You need to ask yourself do you want to be a slave of your own desires or a slave of God?

If you love, trust and obey God, you will get your desires and much more. *Therefore, rely on Him entirely.* You won't be too concerned about fitting in, your biggest concern will become pleasing and obeying Him, and with that comes contentment, peace and happiness.

RESPECT IS YOURS

Respect is not something you should crave. If it isn't given to you then take it forcefully by removing yourself from the disrespectful situation you are in.

KINDNESS

Being kind in this cruel world only adds to your beauty. Your vulnerability makes you valuable. It may sometimes feel like a curse to be able to love and give so much, but let me assure you it is not a curse but a true blessing that not everyone possesses.

GOLD

When you have honesty within you, you will see honesty in others.

When you have a pure and loving heart, you will automatically assume the best of people and believe that they are like you (with no hidden agendas).

Your ability to believe in people does not make you stupid. It makes you Gold. People pretend to be like gold when they are actually rocks, as they start to rust, their true colours are brought to light.

But you were always gold *and you always will be gold* no matter who tries to burn you.

HEALING

Your healing is within you.

You have all the answers to the questions which you have buried in your soul.

So, dig deep and open all the bruises you have put a plaster on. Face your demons, and you will be brave enough to unlock the answers that will finally set your soul *free*.

INSTINCTS

The truth is, when you know- you just know.

Trust your instincts. Don't let them win with their excuses. Don't tolerate their demands by providing evidence.

Instead, ask for proof as to why you should *not* trust your instincts.

BREATHE

When pain comes to revisit you from the past,
breathe it in and then breathe it back out.

SELF-IMPROVEMENT

Get focused on improving yourself and loving yourself until you have no space for negativity.

PREPARED

Love with all you've got, but keep in mind that *nothing* lasts forever. Remind yourself that you will be alright, because you will always have yourself and God to rely on. It will prepare you for anything.

WHAT LOVE IS

Love isn't about suffering or losing yourself to please someone else.

Love is being happy with the person you are, and loving somebody in return who loves your authentic self.

FORGIVE

For the one who oppresses me I respond with forgiveness and prayer for guidance.

THE ONE THAT UNDERSTANDS

It is only you, besides God that understands who you are, what you have been through, how you feel and what it is you desire.

So why not give love to yourself and pray every day until your prayers are answered?

Why would you just hope for the best but not work for the best results?

Understand your greatness and then everybody else will.

YOU ARE YOU

You are not what people say or think. You are *you*, remember that.

DREAM BIG

Do not let people's opinions of what you can achieve make you confused.

Dream big, pray hard and do *you* at your best.

A DIFFERENCE

No matter what job you do or what your role is; it's not trivial. You are making a positive difference to someone or something and that is absolutely everything.

PEOPLE

People will make you feel bad for being you, but *don't let them.*

EXPERIENCE

You will be okay, because you have the ability, the strength and the courage to handle it. All your experiences have taught you this and this you will continue to learn.

RACE

You don't need to be in a race with the rest of the world.

Focus on what makes you happy, and what *you* want in life. Don't let other people tell you what to do or what not to do. Your goals may be different to theirs, but they are still worthy.

What is right for others may not be right for you. Don't let the world make you feel insecure for being you and doing what fulfils *you*.

GROW

It was never about them, it was always about you.
It was about learning and growing from life's
lessons. So don't grieve - grow.

BELONGING

You belong to God and you belong to yourself. Therefore, do not ever feel that you are alone and you do not belong anywhere, because you do.

AFTERWORD

I hope this book brings you closer to yourself and makes you realise the importance of having a healthy and loving relationship with yourself. This book is a gift to me and a gift to you from a part of us we may have once lost.

Made in the USA
Columbia, SC
09 April 2018